INTERACTIVE WORKBOOK

THE POWER

OF

KNOWING

GOD

TONY EVANS

HARVEST HOUSE PUBLISHERS
EUGENE, OREGON

The Power of Knowing God Interactive Workbook
Copyright © 2020 by Tony Evans
Published by Harvest House Publishers
Eugene, Oregon 97408
www.harvesthousepublishers.com

ISBN 978-0-7369-7607-7 (pbk)

21 22 23 24 25 26 27 / BP-SK / 10 9 8 7 6 5 4

CONTENTS

I want to thank my friends at Harvest House Publishers for their long-standing partnership in bringing my thoughts, study, and words to print. I particularly want to thank Bob Hawkins for his friendship over the years, as well as his pursuit of excellence in leading his company. I also want to publicly thank Kathleen Kerr, Betty Fletcher, and Kari Galloway-Marion for their help in the editorial process.

Working with the team at RightNow Media is always a pleasure, and they bring great professionalism and talent to what they do, as well as a love for our Lord. Thank you, Phil Warner, for leading your group so well, and many thanks to the entire team who both filmed and edited this study in Arizona. In addition, my appreciation goes to Heather Hair for her skills and insights in collaboration on this Bible study content and assistance with the video production.

MAKING THE MOST OF THIS INTERACTIVE WORKBOOK

This workbook is a tool to help your group combine the video and subsequent Bible study into a dynamic growth experience. If you are the leader or facilitator of your group, take some time in advance to consider the questions in the Video Group Discussion and Group Bible Exploration portions of this guide and prepare your own personal examples to encourage discussion. In order to ensure your group members get the most out of this study, make sure that each individual has their own Interactive Workbook. This will allow them to take notes during the group time as well as dig deeper on their own throughout the week.

Because every group session includes a video portion, think about the logistics in advance. Will everyone be able to see the screen clearly and hear the teaching? Make sure to position the chairs and set the audio at a comfortable level before the session. You don't want your group to miss anything.

With that in mind, let's preview the guide. Each lesson has six sections:

Video Teaching Notes

Several key points and quotes from the video are provided in this section, but there's also room to write down your own notes.

Video Group Discussion

People can forget the content unless they review it right away. Many of the discussion questions have to do with remembering what the group just viewed. But other questions try to connect the video to the viewers' emotions or experience. *How did you feel when Tony said that? Is that true in your life? Do you have the same issue?*

Group Bible Exploration

This is a Bible study, so each session is grounded in Scripture. Within your group, you may find different levels of faith. This is a time to open up the Bible and grow as a group or help others find their faith.

In Closing

The goal for every Bible study is to apply what you've learned. This section will highlight the main point of the lesson and challenge your group to spend some time in the coming week diving deeper into this week's theme.

On Your Own Between Sessions

This section includes additional study for individuals to keep the content they just learned fresh in their minds throughout the week and to put it into practice.

Recommended Reading

Your group time in this video Bible study will be enhanced if everyone takes the time to read the recommended chapters in *The Power of Knowing God* by Tony Evans. Tony's video teaching follows the book, but the book includes considerably more information and illustrations. If you are the leader, encourage your group to prepare ahead as well.

DO YOU KNOW HIM?

While knowing God does involve your intellect, emotions, and actions, it also involves so much more. Because intellect, emotions, and actions on their own do not comprise the true meaning of knowing.

Consider a husband and wife who have been married for four or five decades. Of course, by then they intellectually know their spouse, they emotionally grasp how he or she makes them feel, and they have made adjustments in their actions in an effort to align with their spouse's desires. However, even with those three aspects of knowing, they may not truly know each other at all.

You've seen them. These couples can predict each other's next word, and they'll dutifully accompany each other to whatever appointment or experience is on the agenda, but something seems to be missing. Despite years together and shared memories, they are still not connected in the way that matters most.

Knowing someone—even knowing God—involves much more than simple knowledge. It involves a connection so authentic and real that it gives birth to a synchronicity and cadence established as a natural outgrowth of the relationship itself. Knowing someone often can't be defined in words or activities. It's that subtle savoring that occurs within two souls uniquely bonded in love.

Our foundational passage for understanding why we are to pursue knowing God intimately is Jeremiah 9:23-24, where we read,

> Thus says the LORD, "Let not a wise man boast of his wisdom, and let not the mighty man boast of his might, let not a rich man boast of his riches; but let him who boasts boast of this, that he understands and knows Me."

When a man sees a lady who captures his imagination, and he walks over to ask her, "What's your name?" he is after much more than information. While information is necessary, that's not his goal. His goal is a relationship. As this man and woman begin to date and start talking on the phone, facts about each other transform into feelings. As these feelings deepen, he becomes moved to ask for her hand in marriage. When she says yes and the wedding occurs, they then spend their first night together on their honeymoon. When the feelings have culminated in a mutual love, they then initiate the full knowing of each other in their first time of intimacy together.

See, that's what the Bible says when we read in Genesis 4:1, "Now Adam knew Eve his wife, and she conceived and bore Cain" (ESV). When the Bible talks about people knowing each other in this biblical sense, it is referring to physical intimacy at its greatest level. This ushers in the ability to both know and be known—which involves much more than mere physical contact and is only attainable in an atmosphere of total and deserved trust.

The Power of Knowing God, pages 12–14

Video Teaching Notes

As you watch the video, use the space below to take notes. Some key points and quotes are provided here as reminders.

Main Idea

- We were created to know God, and we miss out on the fullness of life when we fail to do so. But knowing Him is about more than collecting information. It's about intimacy.

- Many Christians have the right tools (church, community, Bible study) but miss out on an intimate relationship with God.

- God desires that we boast in knowing Him (Jeremiah 9:23-24). There exists a vast difference between head knowledge and heart knowledge. To truly know God, He has to be your greatest desire.

- Moses provides us with an example of desiring to know God (Exodus 33:13-18).

  » He asked to know God's ways (verse 13)

  » He asked for God's presence (verse 15)

  » He asked to see God's glory (verse 18)

- Personal Notes:

Application

Do you want God? Or merely His benefits? God created you to walk in intimacy with Him. Take an honest look at your life and surrender those desires that keep you from that intimacy.

Quotables

- When God says, "I want you to know Me," He says, *I want us to get so close and so intimate that we have come to feel each other, to understand each other, to relate to one another.*

- Every time you bring up the name *God*, along with that name you should bring up the desire to find out more about Him.

- Jesus said this *is* eternal life—that you get to know Him. You get to experience His life pulsating and operating within your life.

Video Group Discussion

1. In the video, Tony touches on rituals people perform in order to know God. He mentioned attending church could be one of those rituals. What are some other activities people participate in that make them feel they are getting to know God when they may just be going through the motions?

2. Tony says in the opening of our study that "God wants to be known relationally, experientially, and intimately." Why is it important to know God in each specific way?

What can we do to increase our ability to know Him in each of these three categories?

3. Take a look at a passage referenced in the video, Jeremiah 9:24 (NIV), and reflect on this Scripture in light of the three ways to know God just mentioned:

Relationally. Read Jeremiah 9:24a:

> Let the one who boasts boast about this: that they have the understanding to know me, that I am the LORD…

How does this portion of the passage reflect knowing God relationally?

Experientially. Read Jeremiah 9:24b:

> …who exercises kindness, justice and righteousness on earth…

Can you share a time when you experienced God's kindness, justice, or righteousness made manifest in your life? What did that experience do to your faith?

Intimately. Read Jeremiah 9:24c:

> …for in these I delight.

The word *delight* reflects emotion. Describe the emotions present in delight.

How does knowing that God is emotionally moved to carry out kindness, justice, and righteousness help you to connect more intimately to Him?

4. In the video, Tony says that knowing God means getting clarity on His character and the work He wants to do on earth. List three ways we can seek to gain clarity on God's character and His work.

   a.

   b.

   c.

   Once clarity on God's character and His work are revealed to us, what can result?

5. Read the following verses. Describe how each relates to our role in carrying out God's works and discuss why knowing God intimately is critical to doing that work well.

   We are His workmanship, created in Christ Jesus for good works, which God prepared beforehand so that we would walk in them (Ephesians 2:10).

   I have come down from heaven, not to do My own will, but the will of Him who sent Me (John 6:38).

   I glorified You on the earth, having accomplished the work which You have given Me to do (John 17:4).

Knowing God fully means His character will ultimately reflect through our own. Yet we cannot have God's character shine through us unless we know Him personally—relationally, experientially, and intimately. Share a specific way you can encourage yourself to pursue knowing God personally this week.

Group Bible Exploration

1. Read the following verses. Explore the *cause* in each passage which then leads to the *effect*—knowing God. Share how each verse describes knowing God as an effect.

   The secret of the LORD is for those who fear Him, and He will make them know [yada] His covenant" (Psalm 25:14).

   Cause:

   Effect:

   "You are My witnesses," declares the LORD, "And My servant whom I have chosen, so that you may know [yada] and believe Me and understand that I am He. Before Me there was no God formed, and there will be none after Me" (Isaiah 43:10).

   Cause:

   Effect:

   I will give you the treasures of darkness and hidden wealth of secret places, so that you may know [yada] that it is I, The LORD, the God of Israel, who calls you by your name" (Isaiah 45:3).

   Cause:

   Effect:

2. Exodus 33 tells about a time when Moses wanted God badly (see verses 13,15,18). Moses had come to know God in a myriad of experiences and had become dissatisfied with a nibble here or there. He was hungry and wanted more.

   Moses was a man who was famished for God. He asked Him repeatedly to remain in close proximity to him so that he could get to know Him. Moses asked God to reveal Himself to him. He practically begged God not to lead him anywhere where He would not also be.

   When you are hungry for someone, you want to be near them. You want to close the distance and remain near them. No matter what the cost. Read the following verses and take notes on what they mean to you personally.

   > As the deer pants for the water brooks, so my soul pants for You, O God. My soul thirsts for God, for the living God; when shall I come and appear before God? (Psalm 42:1-2).

   > Whatever things were gain to me, those things I have counted as loss for the sake of Christ…that I may know Him and the power of His resurrection and the fellowship of His sufferings, being conformed to His death; in order that I may attain to the resurrection from the dead (Philippians 3:7,10-11).

   > I have heard of You by the hearing of the ear; but now my eye sees You; therefore I retract, and I repent in dust and ashes (Job 42:5-6).

3. Hunger for God isn't only about blessings and having Him do things for you. Moses

(Exodus 33), David (Psalm 42:1-2), Paul (Philippians 3:7,10-11), and Job (Job 42:5-6) hungered to know God fully, even in the fellowship of His sufferings. Even if it meant repenting of their own self-will, pride, and previous thoughts. When people experience a shared suffering or mutual struggle, it will often draw them closer together. It creates a greater appreciation for one another on many levels, while developing a deeper intimacy.

> I love those who love me; and those who diligently seek me will find me (Proverbs 8:17).

In what ways does knowing God intimately require participation from us?

How would you feel if someone said they wanted to get to know you but then took no effort to get to know you?

Do you think God ever feels that way about you, or about others in the body of Christ?

In Closing

As you end the study today, spend some time sharing prayer requests related to your pursuit of knowing God and your desire to cultivate your relationship with Him. Be specific about the areas you feel you need to grow in and develop the most. Ask the Holy Spirit to open your hearts throughout this study in order that each of you may come to know God as never before. Also ask that He guard and protect your priorities, time, and passions in order to enable each of you to finish this study in its entirety.

Before session two, complete the "On Your Own Between Sessions" section below. You might want to start the next session by asking people to share what they learned from the exercises on those pages.

On Your Own Between Sessions

1. In the book, Tony goes into greater detail on Moses' pursuit of God and how knowing God was tied to knowing God's character and His ways. He writes,

   > Moses made a very instructive statement when he said, "Let me know Your ways that I may know You." To know God's ways is to know God. To know His ways is to be synced up with what He is doing, aligned with His will and rule. It is to be on the same page with God. See, you can't truly know someone if you don't even know what they are up to. But even though that is true and a reality, many of us miss that. Instead, we make our prayers about us. We word our requests not so He will show us what He is up to and how we can join Him, but more so that we can have our own way. But to know God is to know His ways. Because Moses knew God intimately, God showed him His ways (page 29).

   Read the following Scripture passages:

   > He made known His ways to Moses, His acts to the sons of Israel (Psalm 103:7).

   > As the heavens are higher than the earth, so are My ways higher than your ways and My thoughts than your thoughts (Isaiah 55:9).

   God works in ways that are beyond our own understanding. Why is it important to ask God to show you His ways?

   What are some distractions in your life that might keep you from coming to know God's ways?

What can you do to lessen these distractions?

2. The word *yada* appears more than 1,000 times in Scripture. Tony describes the word this way:

> to know, learn to know
> to be made known, be revealed
> to make oneself known
> to cause to know
> to reveal oneself
> to know by experience

Draw from those descriptions to form your own definition of knowing God.

3. God desires your attention. How does it make you feel to know that He longs for your affection, focus, and time?

Spending your time, energy, and focus on distractions of the world affects your intimacy with God:

> Do you not know that friendship with the world is hostility toward God? Therefore whoever wishes to be a friend of the world makes himself an enemy of God. Do you think that the Scripture speaks to no purpose: "He jealously desires the Spirit which He has made to dwell in us"? (James 4:4-5).

Pray and ask God to enlighten your heart in order to see more clearly any areas of focus that are distracting you from knowing God personally. Seek His heart and wisdom on how to retrain your focus to the pursuit of knowing Him.

4. Life Exercise: Getting Intimate with God.

Identify a time when you can spend concentrated and focused energy on pursuing your understanding and relationship with God each day.

Consider several ways to nurture your relationship with God during this time. It could be writing freely in a journal any thoughts you have toward Him or thanking Him for any of His attributes. Or it could mean looking up Scripture on the attributes of God and meditating on the Scripture for a few minutes each day.

Evaluate how your relationship deepens as you spend consistent time with God. Also evaluate how you are coming to know His various attributes more fully and seeing them shine through your own thoughts, words, and actions.

Repeat. After you've put this into practice this week, seek to repeat it in the weeks to come. You can incorporate the various aspects we are studying about the power of knowing God into your daily intimate time with Him.

Recommended Reading

In preparation for session two, read chapters 3–5 of *The Power of Knowing God.*

SESSION 2

A PATH TO INTIMACY

Back before seat belts, you could always tell when a couple was happy. Happy couples sat together on the driver's side of the car, cuddled up nearly as one. But when couples weren't happy, one person would be on the passenger's side, close to the door, and the other on the driver's side.

As the story goes, one day a husband and wife were driving, and the wife looked over to her husband and said, "We used to sit so close together."

To which the husband replied, "Well, I haven't moved."

If it feels like God is distant, He isn't the one who has moved. It simply means you have moved away from Him.

In Exodus 32, Israel experienced a breakdown in their relationship with God. They made choices which moved them further away from God.

If you are familiar with this story, you will recall that following their miraculous deliverance from slavery, the Israelites built themselves a golden calf to worship. This occurred after they had learned that God had said not to create any idols (Exodus 20:4-5), even if the idol is made with Him in mind.

Yet the Israelites grew frustrated when their leader, Moses, took too long to come back from spending time with God on the mountain. They felt alone. And we all know what happens when you feel alone. It ushers in feelings of helplessness and desperation. The Israelites felt their vulnerability immensely and sought to create something they could touch, see, feel, and have with them at all times.

When God saw what they had done, He became incensed. He was aggravated that the Israelites had so quickly and easily removed themselves from Him by committing this great and terrible sin. Thus, in Exodus 33:3 God told Moses, "Go up to a land flowing with milk and honey; for I will not go up in your midst, because you are an obstinate people, and I might destroy you on the way." That's an interesting statement. He literally told His people to go to the place of blessing, but He would not go with

19

them. The land flowing with milk and honey was their dream, their goal. Evidently it is possible to be physically blessed, yet not have God with you. You can have circumstances going well for you but still be alone.

That's why you cannot look around you at what other people have or what other people are doing and assume they are close to God. Having a blessing does not reveal where someone stands with God in their personal relationship with Him. This principle is laid out for us in Matthew 5:45, which states, "He causes His sun to rise on the evil and the good, and sends rain on the righteous and the unrighteous."

Far too often, people look to the blessing as a validation of God's presence. But when we examine the lives of those in Scripture who were closest to God, we find tribulation, difficulties, and troubles. Being blessed is a wonderful thing, but it is not necessarily an indicator of a person's intimacy with the Lord. Remember, even Satan offered to bless Jesus (Luke 4:5-6). Unfortunately, it is far too easy to assume closeness based on tangible goods alone, which can lead to a level of apathy that stalls the pursuit of God in a believer's life.

God is not a piece of data. Knowing Him isn't akin to knowing how to play a game or manipulate something for your own good. Knowing God is an intense experience that plumbs the very depths of being. It's not about receiving spiritual serendipities or throwing out theological truths that sound good or make you seem like you know Him. Nor is it about amassing spiritual trophies or creating large platforms. Knowing God means sharing a personal relationship with Him.

The Power of Knowing God, pages 37–39

Video Teaching Notes

As you watch the video, use the space below to take notes. Some key points and quotes are provided here as reminders.

Main Idea

- Seeking God is a journey toward Him. You are moving Godward. You are walking on a path that brings you closer in proximity to Him in your thoughts, words, and actions.

- The process of knowing God intimately ought to become an increasingly enjoyable pursuit.

- God desires that you know Him "face to face" (Deuteronomy 34:10).

- We are to be passionate in our approach to knowing God so that we come to know

His heart, character, and ways on a deep, intimate level. This passion will also motivate us to serve and honor Him out of a heart of love rather than duty.

- Personal Notes:

Application

Beware that you do not combine a pursuit of God with the priorities of this world. Pursuing God will often lead to a letting go of previously held priorities or pursuits. Are you willing to pursue Him fully?

Quotables

- It's not just being a Christian; it's pursuing an intimate relationship that will give you that experience of knowing God because you are on fire for the relationship.

- Sometimes sermons can pacify us. Singing can pacify us. Knowledge can pacify us until we wake up and decide we want a meal. We want real food. We want the experience of knowing God.

- I'm talking about something deeper than the 15 or 30 minutes you may spend in the morning in devotions. I'm talking about interacting with God all day long, bringing Him to bear on your decisions, on your thoughts, and in your relationships.

Video Group Discussion

1. Tony begins this session with an illustration about seat belts and how close couples in love used to sit together when they didn't have seat belts. He says, "Intimacy was reflected by closeness." On a scale of 1 to 10, where are you in your intimacy (that is, closeness) with God? In other words, how close would you sit next to Him in a car without seat belts?

1 --- 10

2. In what ways might we hinder the process of getting close to God?

3. What are some things that keep us from sitting close to God? (Some examples might be shame, guilt, apathy, and doubt.)

4. In what ways can we help the process of getting close to God?

5. In the video, Tony gives the illustration of a woman married to an unloving husband who had her complete a list of duties in their home. When her husband died, she married someone who loved and cherished her. She found the old list and realized she was doing everything on it—but not because she was forced to do so. She was motivated by love. Can a loving, deep, abiding, and intimate relationship with God motivate you to serve Him more fully? Why or why not?

On a scale from 1 to 10, where would you rate your motivation to serve God? (1 being "duty" and 10 being "intimacy")

1 --- 10

Describe any parallels or contrasts between your answers on the two scales (question 1 and question 5).

6. How could a greater intimacy with God empower you to live out your life calling and destiny?

Group Bible Exploration

1. Material blessing does not necessarily indicate intimacy with God. This principle is laid out for us in Matthew 5:45: "He causes His sun to rise on the evil and the good, and sends rain on the righteous and the unrighteous." Moses knew this truth. That's why He asked God to go with them into the promised land (Exodus 33:15) when God said He would send them on without Him (Exodus 33:3).

Why do we often mistakenly connect material blessing with God's presence or blessing?

Do you know anyone who calls himself or herself a Christian but is not close to God or honoring to Him? How does it make you feel to see that person prospering? Share why you feel the way you do.

2. Compare and contrast the beginning and end of Psalm 73:

> I was envious of the arrogant as I saw the prosperity of the wicked (Psalm 73:3).

> Whom have I in heaven but You? And besides You, I desire nothing on earth. My flesh and my heart may fail, but God is the strength of my heart and my portion forever. For, behold, those who are far from You will perish; You have destroyed all those who are unfaithful to You. But as for me, the nearness of God is my good; I have made the Lord GOD my refuge, that I may tell of all Your works (Psalm 73:25-28).

What change of heart does the psalmist express regarding his emotions connected to viewing the prosperity of those who do not know God?

What did the psalmist come to value the most as he walked the path to intimacy with God?

How might these lessons impact your path and worldview?

3. Knowing God deeply requires intentionality and honesty (Exodus 33:7-11). It also produces visible change (2 Corinthians 3:2-11). Knowing God deeply may even involve suffering like Christ (Philippians 3:8-11). But in all these experiences, knowing God elevates our emotions above the baseline levels of comparison and jealousy. It elevates our emotions to those known as the fruit of the Spirit.

Listed below are the fruit of the Spirit as found in Galatians 5:22-23. Identify an opposite or opposing emotion or attribute of each and write it in the blanks.

Love   _____

Joy   _____

Peace   _____

Patience   _____

Kindness   _____

Goodness   _____

Faithfulness   _____

Gentleness   _____

Self-control   _____

Which qualities give you more real power to pursue your goals, contentment, and calling?

How does knowing God intimately empower you personally?

4. Read Deuteronomy 34:10 together.

Since that time no prophet has risen in Israel like Moses, whom the LORD knew face to face.

This verse gives us a glimpse into how closely Moses knew God. How do you think Moses' intimacy with God gave him power to accomplish all that he did?

Why is it important to understand the connection between knowing God intimately and His empowerment to live our lives to the fullest (John 10:10)?

What often happens when we seek to perform in our own strength and skills?

5. Read Zechariah 4:6 together.

"Not by might nor by power, but by My Spirit," says the LORD of hosts.

Describe how this verse connects to our empowerment that comes from knowing God intimately.

In Closing

As you end the study today, pray together for a greater understanding of how knowing God intimately strengthens and empowers us in our everyday lives. Ask God for the courage—and restraint—to go to Him first in whatever we face, no matter what, rather than to our friends, the Internet, or even our own thoughts. Talk about ways you can encourage or remind each other to pursue God more fully as part of your daily lives.

Before session three, complete the "On Your Own Between Sessions" section below. You might want to start the next session by asking people to share what they learned from the exercises on those pages.

On Your Own Between Sessions

1. Read the following verses:

> Let me hear Your lovingkindness in the morning; for I trust in You; teach me the way in which I should walk; for to You I lift up my soul (Psalm 143:8).

> It is good to give thanks to the LORD and to sing praises to Your name, O Most High; to declare Your lovingkindness in the morning and Your faithfulness by night (Psalm 92:1-2).

> When I remember You on my bed, I meditate on You in the night watches (Psalm 63:6).

> At night my soul longs for You; indeed, my spirit within me seeks You diligently (Isaiah 26:9).

> In the early morning, while it was still dark, Jesus got up, left the house, and went away to a secluded place, and was praying there (Mark 1:35).

What do these verses tell you about carving time out of your schedule to spend with God?

List seven distinct periods of time or places that you read about in these verses where someone sought God:

1.

2.

3.

4.

5.

6.

7.

Is there any one better time or place to seek God? Why or why not?

2. Let's consider the reasons, emotions, and convictions we may have for seeking to make our time our own rather than using it in pursuit of knowing God. Contrast them with reasons for pursuing God fully.

Reasons to Make Our Time Our Own	Reasons to Pursue God Fully

3. Chapter 5 in *The Power of Knowing God* reminds us that the path to pursuing intimacy with God is often a path littered with pain. But there is a purpose to the pain. We read,

> Now, don't get me wrong. I'm not saying you should go out and look for opportunities to suffer. What I am saying is that when you do encounter suffering, you can recognize it as an invitation to draw near to God. Why? Because there is nothing like knowing God when He brings you through something as only He can do. That's when you get to know Him at another whole level. And that's when you discover the things in you that you need to let go of, the parts that need to die. Becoming like Christ means releasing your sinful propensities and proclivities while embracing His holiness and grace (page 77).

Consider some unhealthy thought patterns, behaviors, or even relationships that might be keeping you stuck on your path to pursuing intimacy with God. List two you would like to surrender to God. Ask Him to remove, change, replace, or simply deal with them.

1.

2.

Take some time to pray through this. Ask God for wisdom on how to let go of the distractions that are holding you back from a full-on pursuit of Him. If you pursue

God and seek to know Him more intimately, what can you expect to see as the outcome in your everyday thoughts, words, and actions?

4. Life Exercise: Meditate Daily

This week, read this excerpt from the book *The Power of Knowing God* once or twice daily. Meditate on different aspects of the concept in this excerpt each day. Take time to write down your thoughts in response to this reading.

Far too many people want a long-distance relationship with God—and only on the good days at that. When it comes to suffering, we are a culture that seeks to avoid it at all costs. But then, we also want to have the resurrection power that comes from God. Yet, without increased intimacy, there can be very little—or even no—supernatural intrusions in life. No breakthroughs. No comebacks. No witnessing heaven brought to bear on earth. None of that comes apart from intimacy with God. This is because His resurrection power is tied to knowing Him in spirit and in truth. It's not tied to just knowing Him from afar; it's tied to knowing Him closely.

And last I checked, there can't be a resurrection without some suffering first. A resurrection takes place only once something is dead. When Paul wrote of "being conformed to His death," he willingly surrendered his rights, goals, and life to God. He literally lived out Romans 12:1, which says, "I urge you, brethren, by the mercies of God, to present your bodies a living and holy sacrifice, acceptable to God, which is your spiritual service of worship."

A "sacrifice" in biblical times was dead. The priest did not place a live animal on the alter, letting it roam around and then taking it down—all the while calling that a "sacrifice." Being a "living and holy sacrifice" is essentially releasing your claim to your will, direction, and purpose while surrendering all to God and His rightful claim on your life…

…Suffering has a way of bringing the best out of people. It also opens up eyes and hearts to a greater level of compassion, understanding, and appreciation than is experienced in seasons of plenty. When we seek to fellowship with Jesus in His sufferings, we are seeking to know Him at a heart level like none other. In visiting His pain through our own, we discover His character and attributes for ourselves. It's more than just reading about them in the Bible. It's coming to know and believe that He is trustworthy, empathetic, authentic, kind, consistent, and caring—even when life is at its worst.

Suffering is an invitation to closeness (pages 74–76).

Consider talking about the thoughts you wrote down when you gather for the next session of *The Power of Knowing God*.

Recommended Reading

In preparation for session three, read chapters 6 and 7 of *The Power of Knowing God*.

KNOW THE UNKNOWABLE

The term *revelation* refers to those moments in our lives where God unveils Himself. He pulls back the curtain and allows us to see Him. Similar to how He passed by Moses in the cleft of the rock, allowing Moses to see Him while also protecting how much he saw, God has given us a way to know and understand Him as much as we are able through the presence and power of the Holy Spirit.

To come to know God, you must come to know Him on a spirit level, which is counterintuitive to how we typically function. We are made up of three parts: body, soul, and spirit. Our body interacts with the physical world through our five senses, which enable us to engage life in the tangible realm. Our soul is the self-life. It is our personhood, which includes our intellect, emotions, and will. And the spirit is the deepest part of us, which has been created to operate in the spiritual realm. It is also the part of us which is able to have contact with God.

Because so much of our lives involve our emotions and the concrete world in which we live, we have come to depend on these aspects of our makeup to guide us through life. Yet when God exposes Himself to us and draws us close for a deep connection with Him, it happens at the spirit level. And it blows our minds. Paul explains,

> We speak God's wisdom in a mystery, the hidden wisdom which God predestined before the ages to our glory; the wisdom which none of the rulers of this age has understood...but just as it is written, "Things which eye has not seen and ear has not heard, and which have not entered the heart of man, all that God has prepared for those who love Him" (1 Corinthians 2:7-9).

This Scripture is not referring to heaven in the sweet by-and-by. No, it is talking about earth in the nasty here and now. It is talking about what can happen in our lives when we come to know God more intimately. When God is interfacing with you on the spirit level, it will involve things that your eyes have never seen. It will involve things that your ears have never heard. It will involve things that your mind could never come up with on its own. Like I said, it will blow your mind.

God is beyond our five senses. His ways are beyond our capacity or ability to conjure up. And yet, we have blocked the knowing of God, or at least limited it, by either our bodies or our souls. As our five senses engage with the world around us, we expect that is how we are to engage with God. So we look for Him in ways we can see, touch, or comprehend. All the while we shut off the connection within our spirit that He longs to make.

Knowing God goes deeper than your physical ability. The experiential knowledge of God involves more than your personhood or senses. It resonates only in the depths of your spirit.

The Power of Knowing God, pages 81–83

Video Teaching Notes

As you watch the video, use the space below to take notes. Some key points and quotes are provided here as reminders.

Main Idea

- By definition, God is unknowable unless He makes himself known. Fortunately, He has done so and gives us His Holy Spirit to lead us into a greater understanding and experience with Him.

- We know God through the Holy Spirit (1 Corinthians 2:6-13). God is Spirit and must be known on his own terms (John 4:24).

- The Holy Spirit helps us understand what God desires for us. The Holy Spirit differentiates the "natural" person from the "spiritual" person (1 Corinthians 2:14-15).

- We grow in our knowledge of God by participating in His work through the Spirit's leading (2 Peter 1:4-7).

- Personal Notes:

Application

Rather than turning to the world for direction, look to God by means of the Holy Spirit within you. Allow Him to deepen your relationship with the Lord through obedience to His Word.

Quotables

- It's the Holy Spirit who gives you the experience with God, and knowing God has to do with experiencing Him, not merely being able to quote doctrines or verses about Him.

- The spiritual person is able to appraise, evaluate, or judge things from God's perspective.

- God's Word tells us what God says and how God thinks…enter the anointing work of the Spirit, turning up the dimmer switch so you see more clearly the personal and specific application that God wants you to know in living it out in your daily experience.

Video Group Discussion

1. In the video, Tony describes the difference between national news and local news. This could be drilled down even further into a neighborhood watch group or social media group where you get alerts about your specific neighborhood. Explain the difference between the *national* and the *local* in your own words. How does that compare to the written Word and the revelation of the Spirit?

2. What is a prominent principle that stood out to you from the video teaching? Take a moment to share why it affected you and how it made you feel.

3. Tony says that the Holy Spirit's job, according to 1 Corinthians 2:7-11, is to turn up the "dimmer switch" on God's Word in order to illumine us to both understand and experience God and His leading in our lives. Can you describe a time when the Spirit did that for you? What was the result?

How should knowing this role of the Holy Spirit affect the way we spend our time with God and His Word?

4. Tony closed the video session by talking about a time when the Holy Spirit lifted a passage off the pages of the Word to let him know God was leading him to pursue the land upon which the church and ministry is now built. What are some other ways the Holy Spirit can lead someone?

Read 1 John 4:1 together.

> Beloved, do not believe every spirit, but test the spirits to see whether they are from God, because many false prophets have gone out into the world.

In light of this caution, how can believers discern direction from the Holy Spirit?

How critical is it to validate the Holy Spirit's leading in your life through alignment with the Word of God? Will the Holy Spirit ever lead a person outside of God's revealed will in Scripture? Why or why not?

Group Bible Exploration

1. Read 1 Corinthians 2:10–11 together:

> The Spirit searches all things, even the depths of God. For who among men knows the thoughts of a man except the spirit of the man which is in him? Even so the thoughts of God no one knows except the Spirit of God.

What is the connection between the Holy Spirit and the thoughts of God?

Can a believer receive divine direction or guidance without the participation of the Holy Spirit? Why or why not?

How critical is it to "walk by the Spirit" (Galatians 5:16) in order to fully live out and experience God's calling and purpose in and through your life?

2. Read together the verses on the following page.

If we live by the Spirit, let us also walk by the Spirit. Let us not become boastful, challenging one another, envying one another (Galatians 5:25-26).

By this we know that we have come to know Him, if we keep His commandments. The one who says, "I have come to know Him," and does not keep His commandments, is a liar, and the truth is not in him; but whoever keeps His word, in him the love of God has truly been perfected. By this we know that we are in Him: the one who says he abides in Him ought himself to walk in the same manner as He walked (1 John 2:3-6).

A new commandment I give to you, that you love one another, even as I have loved you, that you also love one another (John 13:34).

What correlations and similarities do you see among the three passages?

In what practical ways should our walk with the Spirit show up in our everyday thoughts, words, and actions?

3. Tony made an important distinction concerning the order of the words in 1 Thessalonians 5:23. Read the passage together.

Now may the God of peace Himself sanctify you entirely; and may your spirit and soul and body be preserved complete, without blame at the coming of our Lord Jesus Christ.

Why is this order important?

Describe what each term represents and how it helps you carry out God's will in your life.

Spirit:

Soul:

Body:

In Closing

As you end the study today, pray together for a greater closeness with the Holy Spirit. Ask God for insight, for discernment, and for the ability to recognize the Holy Spirit's voice and leading.

Before session four, complete the "On Your Own Between Sessions" section below. You might want to start the next session by asking people to share what they learned from the exercises on those pages.

On Your Own Between Sessions

1. In *The Power of Knowing God*, Tony writes,

> Once you become a Christian, the Holy Spirit invades your human spirit, and the two are merged in such a way that you can now freely receive the things given to you by God. One of the things God gives freely is wisdom and discernment (James 1:5). And one of the things you are to do with that wisdom and discernment is to analyze aspects of life...The spiritually minded person uses an appraisal process to

determine whether the thoughts they are considering are consistent with the Spirit's way of thinking (page 87).

What does it mean to "analyze aspects of life" in order to determine whether they are consistent with the Spirit's way of thinking or the world's?

Have you ever moved forward on what you thought was the Spirit's leading…only to discover later that it was your own inclination? What did you learn from that process?

What specific step can you take this week in order to proactively abide in the Holy Spirit and pursue alignment with God?

2. Read 2 Peter 1:2-7 and John 14:26.

> Grace and peace be multiplied to you in the knowledge of God and of Jesus our Lord; seeing that His divine power has granted to us everything pertaining to life and godliness, through the true knowledge of Him who called us by His own glory and excellence. For by these He has granted to us His precious and magnificent promises, so that by them you may become partakers of the divine nature, having escaped the corruption that is in the world by lust. Now for this very reason also, applying all diligence, in your faith supply moral excellence, and in your moral excellence, knowledge, and in your knowledge, self-control, and in your self-control, perseverance, and in your perseverance, godliness, and in your godliness, brotherly kindness, and in your brotherly kindness, love (2 Peter 1:2-7).

The Helper, the Holy Spirit, whom the Father will send in My name, He will teach you all things, and bring to your remembrance all that I said to you (John 14:26).

What is one of the primary roles of the Holy Spirit in relationship to Jesus?

What are some hesitations you feel about pursuing Christ's attributes and His divine nature above your own?

3. Read 2 Peter 1:8.

    If these qualities are yours and are increasing, they render you neither useless nor unfruitful in the true knowledge of our Lord Jesus Christ.

    What is the intended result of knowing God?

    Describe the phrase "bearing fruit" in your own words, as it pertains to the true knowledge of God.

4. In *The Power of Knowing God,* Tony writes,

    Knowing God involves so much more than reading books about Him or singing songs of praise. While these things are important, they are not the end in themselves. Rather, the qualities of virtue, knowledge, self-control, perseverance, godliness, kindness, and love are the demonstration that the information about God has taken root within you. God has a lot of children who claim to know Him but display little or no fruit. They are still Christians—saved by grace—but little is coming from their lives to bring God glory and advance His kingdom (pages 105–106).

Pray for insight into an area or areas of your life in which you have grown in your demonstration of bearing spiritual fruit. Write it (or them) down. Thank God for the work He's done in your life in bringing you to a greater level of knowing Him.

5. Life Exercise: Participating in your spiritual progress.

   Identify one area in your life where you need more spiritual discernment and guidance.

   Consider how to approach the Holy Spirit for the guidance you need. Ask Him to clarify this for you and to validate His guidance through the Word and other confirmations.

   Evaluate how to proceed once you are certain as to having received the Spirit's guidance.

   Share. After you've put the Spirit's guidance into practice, consider sharing how you felt about the process and what happened as a result. This specific "Life Exercise" may take more than a week to fully experience, but share the results whenever you can—even later on in the study, or after it is over.

Recommended Reading

In preparation for session four, read chapters 8–10 of *The Power of Knowing God*.

HOPE FOR THE HERE AND NOW

When God wanted to reveal Himself at another level to someone in Scripture, it nearly always followed the consistent pattern of crisis. He either allowed or created a crisis. During these times, people would find themselves in situations which they themselves could not fix. They came upon predicaments they could not unravel on their own. They ran into circumstances they could not circumvent. They were in a crisis.

You know you are in a crisis when all your options are gone. When everything you thought could work doesn't work. You can't negotiate your way out of it. You can't spend your way out of it. You can't talk your way out of it. You can't network your way out of it. When all you have learned and tried is not enough to alleviate the situation, you know you are in a God-ordained or God-allowed crisis with a purpose.

More Than You Can Bear

There is a myth in Christianity that I often hear people repeat: "God will not put more on me than I can bear." Maybe you've heard this. Maybe you've said it. Some people even think it's in the Bible. But let me debunk that myth right now with a look at the life of Paul.

In 2 Corinthians, Paul wrote, "We do not want you to be unaware, brethren, of our affliction...that we were burdened excessively, beyond our strength, so that we despaired even of life" (1:8).

If ever there was a hopeless situation, Paul was in it. Paul hadn't done anything to cause it. In fact, he had followed God's leading straight into a place of despair.

If you feel desperate today, you are in good company. The apostle Paul was a man who served God, knew God, and pursued God's calling at all costs. That right there should demonstrate to us that a life of service to our King doesn't guarantee a life without difficulties, sorrow, or sacrifice. In fact, the opposite is typically true.

God sometimes allows situations in your life to appear hopeless because He is trying to direct your focus onto Him. You may feel like giving up because you can't seem to fix the situation, and no one you know can fix it either. All your human resources have been depleted. But Paul reveals a key principle in his next statement: "Indeed, we had the sentence of death within ourselves so that we would not trust in ourselves, but in God who raises the dead...He on whom we have set our hope" (2 Corinthians 1:9-10).

In order to take Paul deeper in faith, God put him in a situation that his abilities and connections could not change. Why? So that Paul would learn to trust God even more so than he had thus far.

The Power of Knowing God, pages 112–113

Video Teaching Notes

As you watch the video, use the space below to take notes. Some key points and quotes are provided here as reminders.

Main Idea

- We often come to know God more personally through a crisis. It is in situations of struggle that He meets us in the here and now with gifts of deliverance, power, and wisdom.

- By knowing God, we enjoy the privileges of His presence when we need it most.

- It can take a crisis to know God on a deeper level.

- God grants us divine power in the times when we need it the most. He sees what we cannot see.

- Personal Notes:

Application

God is greater than any obstacle you face. Turn to Him and trust that He will grant you the deliverance, power, and wisdom you need.

Quotables

- Yes, God will put us in desperate situations. He'll even allow the devil to put us in desperate situations.

- God allows crises because He wants you to get to know Him for the power that He has for the deliverance He can bring by the crisis He allows.

- If you're in a crisis, God has you there to get to know Him, to see some of His attributes at work in things you can't fix, so that you discover, relationally, the God to whom you are legally attached.

Video Group Discussion

1. Read 2 Corinthians 1:9-10 together.

   We had the sentence of death within ourselves so that we would not trust in ourselves, but in God who raises the dead; who delivered us from so great a peril of death, and will deliver us, He on whom we have set our hope. And He will yet deliver us.

   What did Paul say was the reason for the "sentence of death" within them?

   How did Paul need to cooperate with the crisis in order to achieve the spiritual goal intended by it?

   Is it possible to not cooperate with a crisis and wind up becoming hardened and bitter as a result? What does non-cooperation often look like?

2. Read 2 Corinthians 12:8-10 together.

> Concerning this I implored the Lord three times that it might leave me. And He has said to me, "My grace is sufficient for you, for power is perfected in weakness." Most gladly, therefore, I will rather boast about my weaknesses, so that the power of Christ may dwell in me. Therefore I am well content with weaknesses, with insults, with distresses, with persecutions, with difficulties, for Christ's sake; for when I am weak, then I am strong.

Describe a situation when you discovered the power of knowing God through His strength in your own weakness. What did you learn from this experience?

Do you believe that God's strength is enough for times of crisis and struggle? Why or why not?

3. In the video, Tony said the greatest times of knowing God come when there is a contradiction in your crisis. He called this a "catch-22." He spoke about the Israelites leaving Egypt and said, "The Red Sea is before me, and I have no option. You can't go back, can't go forward. When God puts you in a crisis, that's a catch-22. He's creating an opportunity for you to see Him at a level you haven't seen Him before." How should awareness of the spiritual purpose of a "catch-22" affect how you respond in the midst of it?

4. During the video, Tony compares life to a thousand-piece puzzle, a winding road with detours, and the complex intricacies within a watch. Wisdom is needed in order to

navigate life's challenges well. Tony defined wisdom as, "the ability to apply biblical truth to your situation." Read James 1:5 together.

> If any of you lacks wisdom, let him ask of God, who gives to all generously and without reproach, and it will be given to him.

Discuss the process of both seeking and obtaining wisdom.

What are some hindrances to applying wisdom once you've sought and obtained it?

5. Tony concluded the video teaching with an illustration about his son Jonathan's pit bulls. What was your biggest takeaway from that illustration?

Group Bible Exploration

1. Read Ephesians 3:14-19 together.

> I bow my knees before the Father, from whom every family in heaven and on earth derives its name, that He would grant you, according to the riches of His glory, to be strengthened with power through His Spirit in the inner man, *so that Christ may dwell in your hearts through faith; and that you, being rooted and grounded in love,* may be able to comprehend with all the saints what is the breadth and length and height and depth, and to know the love of Christ which surpasses knowledge, that you may be filled up to all the fullness of God.

Based on verse 17 (italicized), what must we allow in order to receive divine power?

What does it mean (in our practical everyday experience) to allow Christ to dwell in our hearts?

2. Read Ephesians 3:20-21 together.

> Now to Him who is able to do far more abundantly beyond all that we ask or think, according to the power that works within us, to Him be the glory in the church and in Christ Jesus to all generations forever and ever. Amen.

What does it mean to have God's power work "within us?" In what ways can we cooperate with the working of this power? And what ways might we work against it?

How does allowing Christ to dwell in our hearts contribute to the level of power that "works within us?"

Can you experience the power working with you without abiding in Christ? Why or why not? Can you share a Scripture passage that supports your answer?

3. Read Ephesians 1:17 together.

> That the God of our Lord Jesus Christ, the Father of glory, may give to you a spirit of wisdom and of revelation in the knowledge of Him.

The Bible connects wisdom and revelation with knowing God. Describe the difference between wisdom and revelation. In what ways do we need both in our lives?

4. Read together Proverbs 1:7.

> The fear of the LORD is the beginning of knowledge; fools despise wisdom and instruction.

What is the beginning of wisdom?

What does it mean to "fear" God?

On a scale of 1 to 10, where would you rate your "fear" of God (1 being least, 10 being most)?

1 -- 10

Now, on a scale of 1 to 10, where would you rate your regular reception of and application of wisdom (1 being least, 10 being most)?

1 -- 10

Is there any correlation between the two graphs?

Despise is a harsh word. We don't always say we "despise" God's wisdom when we choose our own thinking, or when we choose to listen to the media or our friends over God's Word and His Spirit's wisdom. What are some contemporary terms we use to describe passing over spiritual wisdom and God's instruction in place of cultural norms and ways of thinking?

In Closing

As you close your time together, encourage one another to chase after wisdom through allowing Jesus to dwell in your hearts, thoughts, and lives. It is easy to want to give up in the middle of a crisis. Take some time to encourage those in your group who may be struggling and to pray specifically for anyone going through a crisis right now.

Before session five, complete the "On Your Own Between Sessions" section below. You might want to start the next session by asking people to share what they learned from the exercises on those pages.

On Your Own Between Sessions

1. Read Exodus 2:23-24.

> Now it came about in the course of those many days that the king of Egypt died. And the sons of Israel sighed because of the bondage, and they cried out; and their cry for help because of their bondage rose up to God. So God heard their groaning.

What does this passage teach us about crying out to God in times of crisis?

Have you ever avoided crying out to God during struggles, seeking to solve the problem yourself? What did you learn through that process?

Describe the difference between taking questions *to* God and questioning God. Are you willing to allow yourself a greater level of crying out to God and taking Him your questions? Why or why not?

2. In *The Power of Knowing God*, Tony writes,

> While most of us assume all blessings include favor and pleasant circumstances, God shows us that He can also bless us through pain. A downturn in your situation can actually be a blessing which puts you on an upward path...Never look at your crisis as merely a negative situation you must endure. Many crises are positives disguised as pain. They are God reaching into your life and placing you on a pathway to your purpose (page 117).

List three positive results that can arise from a painful crisis in our lives:

1.

2.

3.

3. In *The Power of Knowing God*, Tony writes,

> God is not just after academics. He's after intimacy. And until God is able to expand His presence in you because He's free to roam in all areas of your heart, you will not deepen your intimacy with Him. Intimacy is always based on trust, awareness, and honesty. It is intimacy which releases the Spirit's power in your life (page 132).

In what way does intimacy release the Spirit's power in your life?

What can you do this week to pursue greater intimacy with the Spirit and allow Him to roam free in all areas of your heart?

4. Life Exercise: Discover Power in Pain, Strength in Weakness

This week, be intentional in seeking the power of God—particularly when you face a painful crisis. If you are not in a crisis right now, seek God's power related to a past wound or trauma.

Spend some time meditating on the scriptural principles you have learned through this week's lesson. Allow God's Word to take root in your heart as His Spirit is allowed to roam free. Ask God to give you strength in those areas where you feel weak. If you need to forgive someone but feel too weak to do so on your own, ask God to give you the ability to forgive.

As you continually seek wisdom in the middle of life's struggles, it will become more natural to do on a regular basis. Don't wait until your crisis has grown so large that you are at a loss of what to do. Look to God in the small things too. Let your personal power increase as you discover the process of obtaining both wisdom and strength in the midst of crisis.

Recommended Reading

In preparation for session five, read chapters 11–12 of *The Power of Knowing God*.

THE BENEFITS OF ABIDING

Have you ever seen a pear or an apple struggling and straining to become a pear or an apple? Or how about grapes on a vine? No, none of us have ever seen that. This is because the simple act of abiding brings about the growth of the fruit. It is in your closeness to Christ that fruit is created both in and through your life.

Paul gives us insight into how our relationship with God determines our productivity for God when he says, "We have not ceased to pray for you and to ask that you may be filled with the knowledge of His will in all spiritual wisdom and understanding, so that you will walk in a manner worthy of the Lord, to please Him in all respects, bearing fruit in every good work and increasing in the knowledge of God" (Colossians 1:9-10). In this passage there is a direct connection between bearing fruit and knowing God.

The Greek word for *knowledge* in these verses is *epignosis*. It means "precise and correct knowledge." But what does it mean to have such knowledge of God? Well, this is what we typically think:

> *To know God means you should...*
> *read your Bible.*
> *recite a verse a day to keep the devil away.*
> *go to church.*
> *say a prayer.*
> *take an online course on Scripture or theology.*

That's usually how we interpret what it means to know God. And that's also why so few of us truly live out the full manifestation of His fruit in and through our lives. To know God goes much deeper than informational knowledge alone. It's not just about content. It's about so much more.

In chapter 1 we read about another instance of a word we translate as *knowing*: "Adam knew Eve his wife; and she conceived, and bare Cain" (Genesis 4:1 KJV). The word *knew* in this verse is the Hebrew word *yada*, which means "to know" and "to know by experience" and "to perceive." When Adam knew Eve, it didn't mean he had information about her. No, it meant so much more.

In other words, there was a level of intimacy between them that produced fruit. It bore new life.

To know someone encompasses more than just knowing about them. To truly know someone involves an engagement, interaction, intimacy, and understanding that goes above and beyond cognitive realities. Have you ever seen dancers who spend hours upon hours, days, weeks, and months practicing together so that they know each other's moves and moods through being close to each other? They can anticipate the next step and know how to bring out the best in their dancing partner.

The best linebackers in the NFL are those who have worked so closely together that they can predict each other's moves simply through a shift in weight or a change in the placement of a hand. With crowds roaring and tensions high, these linemen don't have time to talk to the other linemen to find out what they are thinking. But the best players can intuit what their teammates are going to do because they know them that well.

When the apostle Paul talks about knowing God, he's talking about entering into an experiential connection with God. He's talking about knowing Him so deeply, fully, continually, intentionally, and relationally that your every move aligns with His in a cadence of connection. That's what it means to know God. And when you know Him at that level, fruit will be produced. You won't have to force it or fake it; you'll just create it. Or rather, it will be created in you.

The Power of Knowing God, pages 178–180

Video Teaching Notes

As you watch the video, use the space below to take notes. Some key points and quotes are provided here as reminders.

Main Idea

- In addition to meeting our needs, God also grants us the privilege of an identity rooted in His Son and ability to bear spiritual fruit as a result of our abiding relationship with Him.

- By knowing God, we enjoy the privileges of personal identity and personal fruitfulness.

- The world offers many different options for identity. The truth is that our identity is rooted in Christ, but Satan wants to destroy who we are. In Christ, we are a new creation (2 Corinthians 5:17).

- The seed of our identity grows as we apply God's Word to our lives, leading to a deeper relationship with Christ which then bears fruit (Galatians 5:22-24).

- We bear fruit by abiding in Christ (John 15:1-5).

- Personal Notes:

Application

Do you know who you are? Does your life bear the kind of fruit the Bible describes? If you struggle to answer either of these questions, return to your foundation and abide in your Savior.

Quotables

- God wants you to grow in your knowledge of Him so that it becomes an experience with the living and true God.

- If you're going to grow in your knowledge of God, you're going to have to hang out with Him.

- When you hang out with God and when you hang out with your identity in Jesus Christ, He brings about the transformation.

Video Group Discussion

1. Tony compares the outward manifestation of our personal relationship with God to that of a popcorn seed popping due to the internal moisture heating up. What is the internal moisture compared to spiritually?

In what ways can we encourage this internal spark to heat up in our lives?

2. Read Galatians 2:20 together.

> I have been crucified with Christ; and it is no longer I who live, but Christ lives in me; and the life which I now live in the flesh I live by faith in the Son of God, who loved me and gave Himself up for me.

What does this verse tell us about how we are to live our lives? Describe what this looks like in contemporary, everyday terms.

3. In the video, Tony connects the act of bearing fruit to the qualities that show up in actual fruit. He lists three distinct aspects of fruit. List them here:

   1.

   2.

   3.

Describe the types (practical examples) of spiritual fruit which would reflect each of these qualities:

   1.

   2.

   3.

4. Tony mentioned in the video that the term *abide* shows up ten times in the first ten verses of John 15. Read the following verses and share what impact (positive or negative) abiding has, according to the passage.

Abide in Me, and I in you. As the branch cannot bear fruit of itself unless it abides in the vine, so neither can you unless you abide in Me (John 15:4).

I am the vine, you are the branches; he who abides in Me and I in him, he bears much fruit, for apart from Me you can do nothing (John 15:5).

If anyone does not abide in Me, he is thrown away as a branch and dries up; and they gather them, and cast them into the fire and they are burned (John 15:6).

If you abide in Me, and My words abide in you, ask whatever you wish, and it will be done for you (John 15:7).

Just as the Father has loved Me, I have also loved you; abide in My love (John 15:9).

If you keep My commandments, you will abide in My love; just as I have kept My Father's commandments and abide in His love (John 15:10).

Take a moment to pray as a group, asking Jesus to produce supernatural fruit in each of your lives. Ask for Jesus' power to be made manifest as you intentionally draw near Him to abide in Him.

Group Bible Exploration

1. Read Acts 17:24-28 together.

    The God who made the world and all things in it, since He is Lord of heaven and earth, does not dwell in temples made with hands; nor is He served by human hands, as though He needed anything, since He Himself gives to all people life and breath and all things; and He made from one man every nation of mankind to live on all the face of the earth, having determined their appointed times and the boundaries of their habitation, that they would seek God, if perhaps they might grope for Him and find Him, though He is not far from each one of us; for in Him we live and move and exist, as even some of your own poets have said, "For we also are His children."

Far too many people waste an inordinate amount of time trying to discover who they are. They look to their job, their friends, or even their social status and accumulation of stuff. Based on this passage, what is our personal identity connected to and rooted in?

How does getting to know God better allow you to understand and get to know yourself better?

2. Read the following two verses and discuss their connection to our identity:

Seeing that His divine power has granted to us everything pertaining to life and godliness, through the true knowledge of Him who called us by His own glory and excellence (2 Peter 1:3).

You have been born again not of seed which is perishable but imperishable, that is, through the living and enduring word of God (1 Peter 1:23).

What is the source of our life and godliness?

What do you think the "imperishable seed" refers to?

In chapter eleven of *The Power of Knowing God*, Tony explains,

> Once you are saved, the new creation comes to abide within you as a seed. Yet, in order for the seed to realize its full potential, it must grow. For example, a watermelon seed is a very small seed that contains within it an enormous amount of potential for growth. Same with an acorn. Within that seed, which you can hold in the palm of your hand, rests the potential for an oak tree so large it could one day shade an entire house. But it will only do this if it is allowed to grow. If a watermelon seed or an acorn is not allowed to grow, no one will ever experience the potential contained within either of them. Let that concept sink in. As believers in Jesus Christ, we have the divine nature placed within us—but it is placed within us as a seed (page 165).

Is it possible to stifle the growth and expansion of the divine nature planted in us? Why or why not?

3. Read James 1:21 together:

> Putting aside all filthiness and all that remains of wickedness, in humility receive the word implanted, which is able to save your souls.

What must we do in order to fully receive and abide in that which has been planted in us?

Describe what it means to "put aside" things that are damaging, toxic, wicked, or contrary to the will and character of God.

4. According to John 15:7 and James 1:21, we are to abide not only in the presence of God, but also in His Word. Is abiding in the written Word of God a form of abiding in the living Word of God? Why or why not? What does it mean to you to "abide" in the written Word?

In Closing

As you end your session today, spend some time considering the ways we either stifle or encourage the growth of the divine nature within us. Share how personal responsibility is important in spiritual growth, and discuss ways we can intentionally nurture our own spiritual development. Ask God to reveal an approach to each person in the group which will increase the amount of abiding with His Word and His presence.

Before session six, complete the "On Your Own Between Sessions" section below. You might want to start the next session by asking people to share what they learned from the exercises on those pages.

On Your Own Between Sessions

1. God desires for you to know Him in many ways in order to bear much fruit. How do we know that? Because Jesus tells us.

> You did not choose Me but I chose you, and appointed you that you would go and bear fruit, and that your fruit would remain, so that whatever you ask of the Father in My name He may give to you (John 15:16).

You have been chosen to be productive. List three ways you are bearing fruit—being productive for God and advancing His kingdom agenda.

    1. _____

    2. _____

    3. _____

2. Life Exercise: Abide in the Word of God

One way to come to know God more personally is to connect with His Word more regularly.

Be intentional and set aside time each day over the course of the next week to read a specific passage of your own choosing. I recommend reading a whole chapter. But read the same passage or chapter every day for seven days. Each day before you read it, pray that God will prepare your heart to hear from Him.

Write down in a journal or on a smart device the various insights He gives you each day. Revisiting the same passage every day for seven days gives you the opportunity to abide more fully in the written Word of God, increasing your ability to hear from God regarding the meaning and application of His Word.

You may want to spend a moment sharing what you learned from this experience in your group next time you meet.

3. Reflect on the passage below.

> Since the day we heard of it, we have not ceased to pray for you and to ask that you may be filled with the knowledge of His will in all spiritual wisdom and understanding, so that you will walk in a manner worthy of the Lord, to please Him in all respects, bearing fruit in every good work and increasing in the knowledge of God (Colossians 1:9-10).

Take a moment to meditate on the cycle that goes from knowing God to bearing fruit to knowing God:

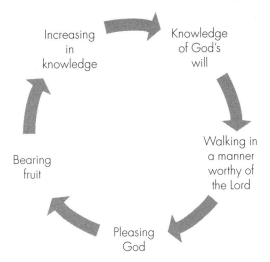

How does this cycle lend itself to continual growth?

In what ways can a person break the cycle?

4. Life Exercise: Abiding and Knowing

How seriously do you take the idea of abiding in the knowledge and understanding of God? Take some serious time to mull over this, to pray, to feel, to be convicted, and to let the presence of God reveal to you where you can be more intentional about knowing Him. Do you need to set aside time for this purpose? Do you need to integrate thoughts about God and communion with Him into your daily activities?

Recommended Reading

In preparation for session six, read chapters 13 and 14 of *The Power of Knowing God*.

EMPOWERED FOR A PURPOSE

The foundational principle for your purpose is this: God created you for Himself. Which is why knowing God intimately is foundational for the fulfillment of your purpose.

You were created for God. You weren't created for yourself.

You were not created so that God can spend all His time trying to figure out how to help you out. God created you for the purpose He has for you—to accomplish His plan for the advancement of His kingdom and for His glory. Any other foundation than this will take you anywhere else but the fulfillment of your purpose.

Scripture tells us that "Enoch walked with God" (Genesis 5:24), not that God walked with Enoch. God is not your copilot; He is in charge. First Corinthians 8:6 states, "For us there is but one God, the Father, from whom are all things and we exist for Him; and one Lord, Jesus Christ, by whom are all things, and we exist through Him."

You exist for God's purposes. Your purpose is His purpose. The Bible doesn't open with, "In the beginning you..." The Bible opens with, "In the beginning God..." (Genesis 1:1). God is the beginning.

The book of Colossians goes deeper into this foundational truth.

> By Him all things were created, both in the heavens and on earth, visible and invisible, whether thrones or dominions or rulers or authorities—all things have been created through Him and for Him. He is before all things, and in Him all things hold together (1:16-17).

Notice that Scripture does not say, "All things have been created through Him and for you." God created all things through Him and for *Him*. That includes you. You have been created for God Himself.

Not only that, but we saw that God is "before all things" as well. He is first. Having a purpose-filled life is all about proper alignment. When God is positioned first in your life, then the next part of that verse holds true for you: "In Him all things hold together."

So if you are unraveling—or if you lack peace, security, stability, and purpose—the first thing you need to ask is what position you are giving God in your life. Because if He is truly before all things in your life, then all things in your life will be held together by Him. But if He is not before all things, then you cannot expect all things to be held together by Him. God has to be positioned *before* all things in order for those things to be held together.

The Central Focus

Why do so many people struggle with stability, calm, and peace and so frequently face a life of emotional, spiritual, or even physical chaos? The answer is simple. Because God has not been positioned before all things for them. He is not first. Instead, He is "in addition to" all things. Or perhaps He comes after trying other things. Yet God will only hold the plan of your life together when He is before all things in your life.

The Power of Knowing God, pages 189–191

Video Teaching Notes

As you watch the video, use the space below to take notes. Some key points and quotes are provided here as reminders.

Main Idea

- With God as our foundation, we become empowered for His purposes and find our place as members of the body of Christ.

- God empowers us for His purposes (Colossians 1:16-17) and can use us for His glory in whatever stage of life we find ourselves.

- God, as Trinity, exists in community. Since we are made in His image, we need community, which we find in the body of Christ.

  » Jesus Christ is the basis for our unity with one another (Ephesians 2:15-22).

  » We are all members of one body (1 Corinthians 12:12-26).

- Personal Notes:

Application

Since we are made in the image of God, we ought to pursue relationships within a local church and seek to live out God's purpose for our lives as members of His body.

Quotables

- If you want to know the plan for your life, don't go looking for the plan. Look for the Planner.

- God wants to get to know you—not informationally, but relationally and intimately. However, He says that decision is in your hands. You must seek Him, pursue Him, run after Him, spend time with Him, communicate with Him, and learn (based on His Word) about Him.

- This isn't only about you. It's much bigger than you. It's about God using you to advance something He is doing in history.

Video Group Discussion

1. Tony mentions that the area the study was filmed in is often known as the "cathedral without walls." Sedona is a place of natural wonders, often evoking worship through its visually stunning landscapes. Why do you think nature can produce worship within us?

   The heavens are telling of the glory of God; and their expanse is declaring the work of His hands (Psalm 19:1).

   In what way can nature "tell of the glory of God"?

   Share about a time when you were led to worship God due to your interaction with or view of nature.

2. In the video, Tony describes different types of relationships with God by comparing them to planets. He says some are "cold," others are "hot," and some are even "hot or cold." What does it mean (in practical, everyday life descriptions) to reflect the following types of relationships?

    Cold:

    Hot:

    Hot or cold:

What are some of the consequences or benefits of living the Christian life in each of those three categories?

    Cold:

    Hot:

    Hot or cold:

3. Tony quotes Jeremiah 29:11 in the video teaching, referring to it as a verse of hope in a very negative book. At the time of the writing, God's people had distanced themselves from God and would be categorized as "cold." Read Jeremiah 29:11-14 as a group.

> "I know the plans that I have for you," declares the LORD, "plans for welfare and not for calamity to give you a future and a hope. Then you will call upon Me and come and pray to Me, and I will listen to you. You will seek Me and find Me when you search for Me with all your heart. I will be found by you," declares the LORD, "and I will restore your fortunes and will gather you from all the nations and from all the places where I have driven you," declares the LORD, "and I will bring you back to the place from where I sent you into exile."

What is the key to moving from a negative experience of life and God toward a positive one of personal purpose and spiritual intimacy?

In your own words, describe what must be done in order for God to "restore" you and set you on the path to your purpose.

Can you think of a biblical example of someone who had grown distant from God but repented, sought Him, and was set on a path to purpose?

In what ways should this story encourage us to keep our eyes on the present and not on our past? In what ways can failures or mistakes in our past keep us from maximizing our spiritual purpose in our present and future?

4. In the video lesson, Tony says, "If you want to know the plan for your life, don't go looking for the plan. Look for the Planner." What does it mean to "look for the Planner?"

When you are considering or pursuing various life purposes and endeavors, do you often go to God or to others first? How does drawing close to God enable you to understand the plan for your life on a greater level?

Group Bible Exploration

1. Like the Israelites during their time in Babylonian captivity, we may also find ourselves as sojourners and exiles on earth. We can wind up in a wilderness or a valley. Read Jeremiah 29:4-7 together.

> Thus says the LORD of hosts, the God of Israel, to all the exiles whom I have sent into exile from Jerusalem to Babylon, "Build houses and live in them; and plant gardens and eat their produce. Take wives and become the fathers of sons and daughters, and take wives for your sons and give your daughters to husbands, that they may bear sons and daughters; and multiply there and do not decrease. Seek the welfare of the city where I have sent you into exile, and pray to the LORD on its behalf; for in its welfare you will have welfare."

What does God says to do when we find ourselves outside of our preferred purpose in life?

In what ways can we seek the welfare of our communities in today's contemporary culture?

What do you think is meant by "in its welfare you will have welfare"?

How does the overall meaning of Jeremiah 29:4-7 connect with the greatest commandments to love God and love others (Matthew 22:37-40)?

2. Read Acts 13:22 and Acts 13:36 together:

> After He had removed [Saul], [God] raised up David to be their king, concerning whom He also testified and said, "I have found David the son of Jesse, a man after My heart, who will do all My will."

> David, after he had served the purpose of God in his own generation, fell asleep, and was laid among his fathers and underwent decay.

David was called a "man after My heart" by God. What did he do with his life in order to demonstrate this closeness with God?

Are you aware of God's purposes for your own life? Share what you believe they are or how you are pursuing their discovery.

3. Read Ephesians 4:11-13 together.

> He gave some as apostles, and some as prophets, and some as evangelists, and some as pastors and teachers, for the equipping of the saints for the work of service, to the building up of the body of Christ; until we all attain to the unity of the faith, and of the knowledge of the Son of God, to a mature man, to the measure of the stature which belongs to the fullness of Christ.

What is the overall principle in these verses?

Why is it important to live intentionally in Christian community and pursue your role in it?

In what ways are you or do you need to use your gifts in order to build up the body of Christ?

How do you feel when you've used your spiritual gifts to help someone else? Why do you think you feel this way?

4. Read Galatians 6:10 together.

While we have opportunity, let us do good to all people, and especially to those who are of the household of the faith.

What does it mean (in practical, everyday examples) to "do good?"

To whom are we each to do good?

Why do you think Paul emphasized "especially to those who are of the household of the faith"?

In what ways can your group set about to intentionally "do good" for the members in your group, as well as those outside of your group? Identify three practical activities you can do.

1.

2.

3.

In Closing

As you end this study, keep these truths at the front of your mind.

1. You can access the power of God through your relational intimacy with God.

2. Rather than seeking to live in your own power, rely on the One who supplies all.

3. Seek to cultivate intimacy with God through time spent in His Word and meditating on His truths and attributes.

4. Break out of your comfort zone and get to know God more fully through new experiences with Him.

5. Once you've confirmed it in His Word, act on what He tells you to do.

6. Abide in Jesus.

7. Honor Him by living out the purpose He has for you individually and in community.

You have all the power you need to fully live out the abundant life Christ came to give you. But you need to tap into that power through a close relationship with God. Start there. Seek Him. Then watch Him reveal Himself to you in amazing ways. You can live a life on purpose for His glory and the advancement of His kingdom on earth.

THE URBAN ALTERNATIVE

The Urban Alternative (TUA) equips, empowers, and unites Christians to impact individuals, families, churches, and communities through a thoroughly kingdom-agenda worldview. In teaching truth, we seek to transform lives.

The core cause of the problems we face in our personal lives, homes, churches, and societies is a spiritual one. Therefore, the only way to address that core cause is spiritually. We've tried a political, social, economic, and even a religious agenda, and now it's time for a kingdom agenda.

The kingdom agenda can be defined as the visible manifestation
of the comprehensive rule of God over every area of life.

The unifying central theme throughout the Bible is the glory of God and the advancement of His kingdom. The conjoining thread from Genesis to Revelation—from beginning to end—is focused on one thing: God's glory through advancing God's kingdom.

When we do not recognize that theme, the Bible becomes for us a series of disconnected stories that are great for inspiration but seem to be unrelated in purpose and direction. Understanding the role of the kingdom in Scripture increases our understanding of the relevancy of this several-thousand-year-old text to our day-to-day living. That's because God's kingdom was not only then; it is now.

The absence of the kingdom's influence in our personal lives, family lives, churches, and communities has led to a deterioration in our world of immense proportions:

- People live segmented, compartmentalized lives because they lack God's kingdom worldview.

- Families disintegrate because they exist for their own satisfaction rather than for the kingdom.

- Churches are limited in the scope of their impact because they fail to comprehend that the goal of the church is not its existence but its influencing the world for the kingdom.

- Communities have nowhere to turn to find real solutions for real people who have real problems because the church has become divided, ingrown, and unable to transform the cultural and political landscape in any relevant way.

By optimizing the solutions of heaven, the kingdom agenda offers us a way to see and live life with a solid hope. When God is no longer the final and authoritative standard under which all else falls, order and hope have left with Him. But the reverse is true as well: If God is still in the picture, and as long as His agenda is still on the table, we have hope. Even if relationships collapse, God will sustain us. Even if finances dwindle, God will keep us. Even if dreams die, God will revive us. As long as God and His rule are still the overarching standard in our lives, families, churches, and communities, hope remains.

Our world needs the King's agenda. Our churches need the King's agenda. Our families need the King's agenda.

We've put together a three-part plan to direct us to heal the divisions and strive for unity as we move toward the goal of truly being one nation under God. This three-part plan calls us to assemble with others in unity, to address the issues that divide us, and to act together for social impact. Following this plan, we will see individuals, families, churches, and communities transformed as we follow God's kingdom agenda in every area of our lives. You can request this plan by emailing info@tonyevans.org or by going online to tonyevans.org.

In many major cities, drivers can take a loop to the other side of the city when they don't want to head straight through downtown. This loop takes them close enough to the city center so they can see its towering buildings and skyline but not close enough to actually experience it.

This is precisely what we, as a culture, have done with God. We have put Him on the "loop" of our personal, family, church, and community lives. He's close enough to be at hand should we need Him in an emergency but far enough away that He can't be the center of who we are. We want God on the "loop," not the King of the Bible who comes downtown into the very heart of our ways. And as we have seen in our own lives and in the lives of others, leaving God on the "loop" brings about dire consequences.

But when we make God and His rule the centerpiece of all we think, do, or say, we experience Him in the way He longs for us to experience Him. He wants us to be kingdom people with kingdom minds set on fulfilling His kingdom's purposes. He wants us to pray, as Jesus did, "Not my will, but Thy will be done" because His is the kingdom, the power, and the glory.

There is only one God, and we are not Him. As King and Creator, God calls the shots. Only when we align ourselves under His comprehensive hand do we access His full power and authority in all spheres of life: personal, familial, ecclesiastical, and government.

As we learn how to govern ourselves under God, we then transform the institutions of family, church, and society using a biblically based kingdom worldview.

Under Him, we touch heaven and change earth.

To achieve our goal, we use a variety of strategies, approaches, and resources for reaching and equipping as many people as possible.

Broadcast Media

Millions of individuals experience *The Alternative with Dr. Tony Evans*, a daily broadcast on nearly 1,400 radio outlets and in over 130 countries. The broadcast can also be seen on several television networks and is available online at tonyevans.org. As well, you can listen to or view the daily broadcast by downloading the Tony Evans app for free in the App Store. Over 30,000,000 message downloads/streams occur each year.

Leadership Training

The *Tony Evans Training Center* (TETC) facilitates a comprehensive discipleship platform, which provides an educational program that embodies the ministry philosophy of Dr. Tony Evans as expressed through the kingdom agenda. The training courses focus on leadership development and discipleship in the following five tracks:

- Bible & Theology
- Personal Growth
- Family and Relationships
- Church Health and Leadership Development
- Society and Community Impact Strategies

The TETC program includes courses for both local and online students. Furthermore, TETC programming includes course work for non-student attendees. Pastors, Christian leaders, and Christian laity—both local and at a distance—can seek out the Kingdom Agenda Certificate for personal, spiritual, and professional development. For more information, visit tonyevanstraining.org.

Kingdom Agenda Pastors (KAP) provides a viable network for like-minded pastors who embrace the kingdom agenda philosophy. Pastors have the opportunity to go deeper with Dr.

Tony Evans as they are given greater biblical knowledge, practical applications, and resources to impact individuals, families, churches, and communities. KAP welcomes senior and associate pastors of all churches. KAP also offers an annual KAP Summit each year in Dallas with intensive seminars, workshops, and resources. For more information, visit: kafellowship.org

Pastors' Wives Ministry, founded by Dr. Lois Evans, provides counsel, encouragement, and spiritual resources for pastors' wives as they serve with their husbands in the ministry. A primary focus of the ministry is the KAP Summit, where senior pastors' wives are offered a safe place to reflect, renew, and relax, along with training in personal development, spiritual growth, and care for their emotional and physical well-being. For more information, visit loisevans.org.

Kingdom Community Impact

The outreach programs of The Urban Alternative seek to provide positive impact on individuals, churches, families, and communities through a variety of ministries. We see these efforts as necessary to our calling as a ministry and essential to the communities we serve. With training on how to initiate and maintain programs to adopt schools; provide homeless services; and partner toward unity and justice with the local police precincts, which creates a connection between the police and our community, we, as a ministry, live out God's kingdom agenda according to our *Kingdom Strategy for Community Transformation*.

The *Kingdom Strategy for Community Transformation* is a three-part plan that equips churches to have a positive impact on their communities for the kingdom of God. It also provides numerous practical suggestions for how this three-part plan can be implemented in your community, and it serves as a blueprint for unifying churches around the common goal of creating a better world for all of us. For more information, visit tonyevans.org, then click on the link to access the 3-Point Plan.

The *National Church Adopt-a-School Initiative* (NCAASI) prepares churches across the country to impact communities by using public schools as the primary vehicle for effecting positive social change in urban youth and families. Leaders of churches, school districts, faith-based organizations, and other nonprofit organizations are equipped with the knowledge and tools to forge partnerships and build strong social service delivery systems. This training is based on the comprehensive church-based community impact strategy conducted by Oak Cliff Bible Fellowship. It addresses such areas as economic development, education, housing, health revitalization, family renewal, and racial reconciliation. We assist churches in tailoring the model to meet specific needs of their communities while simultaneously addressing the spiritual and moral frame of reference. Training events are held annually in the Dallas area at Oak Cliff Bible Fellowship. For more information, visit churchadoptaschool.org.

Athlete's Impact (AI) exists as an outreach both into and through the sports arena. Coaches can be the most influential factor in young people's lives, even ahead of their parents. With the growing rise of fatherlessness in our culture, more young people are looking to their coaches for guidance, character development, meeting practical needs, and hope. Athletes fall just after coaches on the influencer scale. Whether professional or amateur, they influence younger athletes and kids within their spheres of impact. Knowing this, we aim to equip and train coaches and athletes on how to live out and utilize their God-given roles for the benefit of the kingdom. We aim to do this through our iCoach App as well as through resources such as *The Playbook: A Life Strategy Guide for Athletes*. For more information, visit icoachapp.org.

Tony Evans Films ushers in positive life change through compelling video-shorts, animation, and feature-length films. We seek to build kingdom disciples through the power of story; use a variety of platforms for viewer consumption and have more than 100,000,000 digital views; and merge video-shorts and film with relevant Bible study materials to bring people to the saving knowledge of Jesus Christ and to strengthen the body of Christ worldwide. Tony Evans Films released its first feature-length film, *Kingdom Men Rising*, in April 2019 in over 800 theaters nationwide and in partnership with Lifeway Films. The second release, *Journey with Jesus*, is in partnership with RightNow Media.

Resource Development

By providing a variety of published materials, we are fostering lifelong learning partnerships with the people we serve. Dr. Evans has authored more than 125 unique titles based on over 50 years of preaching—in booklet, book, or Bible-study format. He also holds the honor of writing the first full-Bible commentary by an African American. *The Tony Evans Study Bible* was released in 2019, and it sits in permanent display as a historic release in the Museum of the Bible in Washington, D.C.

For more information and a complimentary copy of Dr. Evans's devotional newsletter, call (800) 800-3222; write to TUA at P.O. Box 4000, Dallas, TX, 75208; or visit us online at: www.tonyevans.org

YOUR *Eternity* IS OUR *Priority*

At The Urban Alternative, eternity is our priority—for the individual, the family, the church and the nation. The 45-year teaching ministry of Tony Evans has allowed us to reach a world in need with:

The Alternative – Our flagship radio program brings hope and comfort to an audience of millions on over 1,300 radio outlets across the country.

tonyevans.org – Our library of teaching resources provides solid Bible teaching through the inspirational books and sermons of Tony Evans.

Tony Evans Training Center – Experience the adventure of God's Word with our online classroom, providing at-your-own-pace courses for your PC or mobile device.

Tony Evans app – Packed with audio and video clips, devotionals, Scripture readings and dozens of other tools, the mobile app provides inspiration on-the-go.

**Explore God's kingdom today.
Live for more than the moment.
Live for *eternity*.**

tonyevans.org

Life is busy,
but Bible study is still possible.

a **portable** seminary

Explore the kingdom.
Anytime, anywhere.

TONY EVANS
TRAINING CENTER

tonyevanstraining.org

To learn more about Harvest House books and
to read sample chapters, visit our website:

www.harvesthousepublishers.com

HARVEST HOUSE PUBLISHERS
EUGENE, OREGON